WISE
CHOICES

CW00338878

SIX–DAY CREATION

Does it matter what you believe?

ROBERT J.M. GURNEY

*'Get wisdom, get understanding; do not forget my words or
swerve from them.
Do not forsake wisdom, and she will protect you; love her, and
she will watch over you.
Wisdom is supreme; therefore get wisdom.
Though it cost you all you have, get understanding.'*

Proverbs 4:5–7

I am grateful to Dr Don Batten and Dr Arthur Jones for reading the manuscript of this book and making a number of helpful suggestions.

All Scripture quotations are taken from the New King James Version

A CIP record is held at The British Library   ISBN 978–1–84625–097–2

Published by Day One Publications Ryelands Road, Leominster, HR6 8NZ

Tel 01568 613 740 FAX 01568 611 473   email—sales@dayone.co.uk www.dayone.co.uk

Tel In North America call 888–329–6630

Editor: Suzanne Mitchell

Illustrations: Susan LeVan and Bradley Goodwin   Printed by TJ International Ltd

Dr Robert Gurney provides a succinct and important argument in favour of a literal reading of Genesis 1–11. This book includes scientific and theological discussions, but majors on how the biblical account of creation should be interpreted. Gurney argues for a grammatical-historical hermeneutic, which recognizes metaphor and poetry etc., but at the same time accepts the literal nature of the account. As a former medical missionary, Gurney argues that a correct understanding of biblical origins is essential for effective evangelism and for upholding Christian values.

—Andrew M. Sibley BSc (Hon), MSc EDM (Open), FRMetS. Council member of the Creation Science Movement and author of Restoring the Ethics of Creation

Dr Gurney writes out of personal experience of having tried to accommodate his understanding of the Bible to modern science's creation myth. Having eventually seen the futility of this, he embraced the historicity of the Genesis account and discovered a whole new way of looking at things that just made sense. Like a reformed smoker, he is passionate about countering the destructive effects of the accommodation he attempted. But it is a reasoned passion and the reader of this short treatment will be encouraged and challenged. The author has provided a valuable introduction to the matters of greatest importance in this crucial debate, upon which, I believe, hinges the very survival of a Christian witness in many once-Christian nations. Heartily recommended!

—Don Batten B.Sc.Agr.(Hons 1), Ph.D., senior writer, researcher and lecturer, Creation Ministries International (Australia), Brisbane, Australia

Here is a book I can commend to the Christian and non-Christian alike. It is an excellent introduction to the creation/evolution debate and shows that this question is about authority—the authority of the Bible versus the authority of the scientist and his evolutionary interpretations of origins. Sub-titled *Does it matter what you believe?* the author shows that it does matter what you believe about origins. Get it wrong and you end up with a society that does not believe in God and where there is breakdown of family life, sexual immorality, and a lack of respect for the sanctity of human life. Recognize this description of Western Society? It is my hope that people who read this book will realize the importance of the creation debate and will recognize that what we are reaping in our society is the result of uncritically accepting evolution as the explanation of why we are here.

—A J Monty White BSc, PhD [Wales], CChem, MRSC, Chief Executive, Answers in Genesis (UK/Europe)

CONTENTS

GUIDE TO SOME TERMS USED

Carnivory: Carnivorous behaviour. The eating of animal flesh.

Concordism: A method of harmonizing the Bible with the secular view of origins which attempts to preserve the historicity of the biblical account of creation.

Day-age theory: A concordist theory which proposes that the 'days' of creation in Genesis 1 were vast ages.

Discordism: A method of harmonizing the Bible with the secular view of origins which regards the biblical account of creation as non-historical.

Gap theory: A concordist theory which proposes that there is a gap, millions of years long, between the first two verses of Genesis 1. Most of the fossils and rock layers are the remains of a previous creation which was destroyed by a great flood. Verses 3–31 describe a reconstruction of the world in six literal days.

Literary framework interpretation: A discordist theory which proposes that Genesis 1 is theological, not chronological. It is a stylized literary construction which is not meant to be taken as literal history.

Macro-evolution: The hypothetical 'molecules-to-man' kind of evolution. The hypothesis that inorganic matter developed into a simple form of life, and then, over millions of years, into all the more complex forms of life, including man. It would require huge increases of genetic information.

Micro-evolution: The limited changes in living things which can be observed taking place around us today. Better described as 'variation' or 'diversification'. There is no increase of genetic information. Very often there is loss of genetic information.

Uniformitarianism: The assumption that the natural processes operating in the past are the same as those that can be observed operating in the present. Often summarized in the statement: 'The present is the key to the past'.

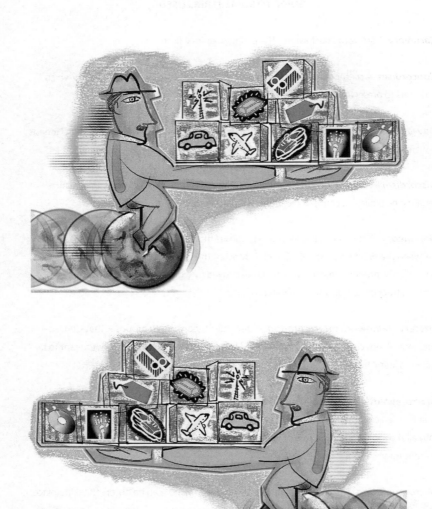

Introduction

In today's world, Christians have to face the fact that there is a conflict, real or apparent, between the biblical account of creation and a theory of origins which is believed by the majority of scientists. It is a theory which is constantly presented to us, in education and in the media, as scientific fact. I refer, of course, to the theory of evolution, with its associated billions of years. On the one hand, the Bible appears to say that God created the world and universe in six days a little over 6000 years ago, and God saw that his new creation was 'very good'. It was only when Adam and Eve disobeyed God that evil (both moral and physical) came into the world. Secular scientists, on the other hand, believe that the universe is billions of years old, and that the history of life on earth is one of millions of years of death, disease, suffering, struggle and violence. In fact, many Christians believe this too.

Does it matter?

Does it matter? Is it important? Many Christians think it is not. 'It is just a side issue,' they say. 'Let's just get on with the job of evangelism and practical Christianity.' 'There are more important things to spend time on than a divisive debate about creation and evolution.' It is probably true that most Christians in the UK ignore this debate or are unaware of it, or hold some kind of 'old-earth' view. Yet many of them are godly people who live fruitful Christian lives. Clearly our salvation and sanctity do not depend on whether or not we believe that God created the heavens and the earth in six literal days. Nevertheless, when we look at the big picture, it is clear that this debate is actually very important. I intend to show in this book that the theory of evolution with its associated billions of years

- is incompatible with Scripture;
- attacks the foundations of Christian doctrine;
- was originated by deists and atheists whose intention was to exclude God from science;
- is the foundational belief of secular humanism—not to mention Marxism, Nazism and other ideologies;
- has borne much evil fruit in the lives of people and nations;

- is scientifically incorrect;
- is a satanic deception.

I believe that the church in the Western world has made a disastrous mistake in trying to fuse Christianity with the secular view of origins. I believe also that the catastrophic decline of Christianity and the rise of secular humanism in the West have been caused partly by this very mistake. F. Sherwood Taylor, Curator of the Museum of the History of Science, Oxford, said this: '… I myself have little doubt that in England it was geology and the theory of evolution that changed us from a Christian to a pagan nation.'[1]

Some Christians do not take kindly to statements of this nature. They are annoyed and impatient with 'young-earth' creationists, especially when the latter say that 'old-earth' creationists are compromising with a satanic deception. But if the secular view of origins really *is* a satanic deception, it *must* be exposed and rejected. It would not be right to sit back and say that it is simply a matter of my opinion versus your opinion. We are, after all, commanded to 'test all things' (1 Thessalonians 5:21). When young-earth creationists reject evolutionary and old-earth teaching, they are accused of being uncharitable, divisive, simplistic and irrational, and of refusing to face the facts of science. This brings us to the heart of the matter.

The central issue at stake here is not whether the earth and universe were created in six days a few thousand years ago, *it is the authority of God's Word.* Do we believe that the Bible is the infallible, inerrant word of God, and that it is supremely authoritative in everything it says? If so, are we prepared to submit to its authority and believe it, even when it contradicts majority scientific opinion? If the plain meaning of Scripture (discussed later) is at odds with majority scientific opinion, do we question the truth of what the scientists tell us, or do we question the truth of what God has revealed to us? Do we reinterpret the scientific evidence, or do we reinterpret Scripture?

I think it is true to say that, in the Western world, the majority of Christian leaders have accepted the secular view of origins—the billions of years, if not the theory of evolution—and have reinterpreted Scripture to fit in with this view. In effect, I believe, they have (unintentionally) put the authority of 'science' above the authority of Scripture. Instead of beginning with *the infallible, unchanging Word of God who was there* and interpreting the scientific evidence in the light of that Word, they begin with *a fallible, changing opinion of men who were not there* and interpret Scripture in the light of that opinion. (Note that majority scientific opinion is not scientific fact. Many discarded theories were once majority opinion.) Again and again various evangelical leaders have admitted that when Genesis 1 is taken in a straightforward way, it appears to teach that the universe was created in six ordinary days. But then they go on to say that this cannot be its true meaning, because science has proved that the universe is millions or billions of years old.

Three examples

I will give three examples of this. The first is Charles Hodge (1797–1878), who was a systematic theologian at Princeton Theological Seminary. He wrote many books and articles defending the truths of Christianity, including biblical inerrancy. But he lapsed when he rejected the plain meaning of Genesis because of alleged geological facts. Actually they were not facts at all—they were uniformitarian *interpretations* of facts. (Uniformitarianism is the assumption that the natural processes operating in the past are the same as those that can be observed operating in the present. It discounts, for example, the possibility of the global Flood of Noah.) This is what he wrote: 'It is of course admitted that, taking this account [Genesis] by itself, it would be most natural to understand the word [day] in its ordinary sense; but if that sense brings the Mosaic account into conflict with facts [millions of years], and another sense avoids such conflict, then it is obligatory on us to adopt that other.'[2]

My second example is the evangelical theologian Gleason L. Archer: 'From a superficial reading of Genesis 1, the impression would seem to be that the entire creative process took place in six twenty-four-hour days … this seems to run counter to modern scientific research, which indicates that the planet Earth was created several billion years ago …'[3]

My third example is this. Not long ago, I had a debate, conducted by e-mail, with a certain evangelical leader. At first he argued that the days of creation could not have been literal days because the sun was created on the fourth day, and he pointed out that in the Bible the word 'day' can have a figurative meaning, etc., etc. He also emphasized that science has proved that the world and universe are billions of years old. However, I sent him an article (now published as a booklet) entitled '15 Reasons to Take Genesis as History'.[4] The article showed that the days of creation are clearly meant to be understood as literal days, and that grammatically, the creation account is consecutive, historical narrative—not poetry or metaphor. After reading it, the leader wrote, 'With regard to the "15 Reasons" article I have no problem with his argument regarding the internal witness of Scripture.' He also wrote that he had 'no problem with James Barr'. James Barr was a leading Hebrew scholar and professor at Oxford University, and was quoted as follows in the '15 Reasons' article:

> … probably, so far as I know, there is no professor of Hebrew or Old Testament at any world-class university who does not believe that the writer(s) of Gen. 1–11 intended to convey to their readers the ideas that:
>
> a) creation took place in a series of six days which were the same as the days of 24 hours we now experience;
>
> b) the figures contained in the Genesis genealogies provide by simple addition a chronology from the beginning of the world up to later stages in the biblical story;
>
> c) Noah's Flood was understood to be worldwide and extinguish all human and animal life except for those on the ark.[5]

Apparently this evangelical leader accepted James Barr's statement, and he accepted the '15 Reasons' argument concerning what the Bible intends us to understand—although it contradicted what he himself had been saying. But in spite of this, he continued to insist that the world and universe must be billions of years old, because it is 'a proven fact of science'. How did he reconcile these contradictory positions? His solution was to describe the biblical teaching as 'the internal witness of Scripture'. In other words, he was saying—if I understand him correctly—that the biblical version of creation and the Flood is purely 'internal', and has little or nothing to do with external reality.

He was, in fact, embracing the liberal belief that Scripture is authoritative in the realm of 'spiritual' things, but not in the realm of history and science. He was accepting that the Bible says one thing, and that secular science says something entirely different—and was concluding that, when it comes to the physical reality of creation, we must believe secular science rather than the Bible. As an evangelical, he would probably say that he believes the Bible is inerrant in all areas, including history and science. But as far as creation is concerned, I think it is clear that he is not putting that belief into practice.

Different positions
Many evangelicals in the West think along the following lines: The Bible *appears* to say that God created the universe in six literal days just over 6000 years ago, and that the Flood was global. But science has proved evolution and/or billions of years; therefore the Bible does not mean what it *appears* to say. They remember the Galileo affair. They remember that some Christians refused to believe that the solar system is heliocentric, because they thought (wrongly) that the Bible says it is geocentric. They fear that they would be making the same kind of mistake if they were to reject evolution and/or billions of years. Therefore they have invented various theories which try to harmonize the Bible with evolution and/or billions of years. They search for evidence to prove that the Bible does not really mean what it *appears* to say.

Ironically, non-evangelical Hebrew scholars like James Barr may be better judges of what the author intended us to understand. They are not worried about trying to harmonize the creation account with science, because they do not believe in the inerrancy of Scripture. They are free to concentrate solely on *what the text actually says.* As Hebrew scholars, they have no doubt whatsoever that the author intended us to understand that God created the universe in six literal days a few thousand years ago, and that Noah's Flood was worldwide. Young-earth creationists agree that this is what the text says, and is what the author intended us to understand. The difference is that *we believe it!*

A change of position

I understand the thought processes of 'old-earth creationists' because I myself was one of them until quite recently! I was convinced that science has proved that the universe is billions of years old. In various ways I tried to reconcile the secular timescale of origins with the biblical account of creation. I tried 'progressive creation' (repeated episodes of creative activity over millions of years), the 'literary framework' theory (in which the whole account is symbolical) and finally a theory of my own invention! In the end I realized I was twisting and turning, trying to get round the clear, unambiguous teaching of Scripture. Also, my eyes were opened to the fact that the scientific *evidence* (as opposed to the secular interpretation of that evidence) actually favours the biblical account. I have come to believe that I was compromising. At the time, however, I sincerely believed that I was *not* compromising.

I have the highest regard for evangelical scholars; but I believe that many of them (and many other Christians) have gone down the wrong path by trying to harmonize the biblical account of creation with the secular view of origins. Incidentally, those of us who believe that Genesis 1–11 is meant to be understood as straightforward history prefer to call ourselves 'biblical creationists', not 'young-earth creationists'.

Notes

1. **F. S. Taylor,** 'Geology Changes the Outlook', in *Ideas and Beliefs of the Victorians* (London: Sylvan Press, 1949), p. 195—one of a series of talks broadcast on BBC radio.

2. **C. Hodge,** *Systematic Theology* (Grand Rapids, MI: Eerdmans, 1997), pp. 570–571.

3. **G. L. Archer,** *A Survey of Old Testament Introduction* (Chicago: Moody Press, 1994), pp. 196–197.

4. **D. Batten and J. Sarfati,** *15 Reasons to Take Genesis as History* (Brisbane: Creation Ministries International, 2006).

5. **J. Barr,** Letter to David C. C. Watson, 23 April 1984.

History

In the rest of this book, I will discuss the question of how God created the heavens and the earth under five headings—History, The Bible, Old-earth theories, Problems and Science. In this section I will take a brief look at how the Christian church has dealt with this question. I will look also at the origins of the modern theory of evolution, with its timescale of billions of years, and at some of the consequences. We could call them the *roots* and *fruits* of these beliefs.

Past interpretations

How has Genesis 1–11 been interpreted by Christians in the past? Jonathan Sarfati deals with this question in depth in Chapter 3 of his book *Refuting Compromise*.[1] His treatment includes lengthy quotations from the Church Fathers, the Reformers, the Westminster Confession of Faith (1646), John Wesley and others. Nearly all those who were specific about the days of creation accepted that God created the world and universe in six literal days. Among the Early Church Fathers, the only exceptions found were Clement of Alexandria (c.150–215), Origen (185–253) and Augustine (354–430).[2] But all three were from the Alexandrian school, and so tended to allegorize various passages of Scripture. Their allegorization did not arise from within the text, but from outside, Greek influences. In any case, they said that God created everything in an instant, not over long periods of time. Furthermore, they argued explicitly for the biblical timeframe of a few thousand years, as well as the global Flood of Noah. (Augustine, incidentally, had no knowledge of Hebrew.) The following quotation concerns the Church Fathers of the Eastern Orthodox (EO) church:

> The late Seraphim Rose, an EO priest, meticulously documented the views of the church fathers of the EO church, showing that they viewed Genesis the way modern creationists do.[3] ... Rose showed how the EO church fathers were unanimous in their view of the historicity of creation week, the Fall and the global Flood. They also believed that God's creative acts were *instantaneous*. They saw the world before the Fall as fundamentally and profoundly different to that which pertained after the Fall.[4]

The Jewish philosopher Philo of Alexandria (c. 20 BC–AD 50) favoured a figurative interpretation; but he was a Hellenized Jew, and he used allegory to fuse and harmonize Greek philosophy and Judaism. Until later years, medieval theologians (c. 600–1517) tended to follow Augustine; but some, including Thomas Aquinas, rejected his view and interpreted Genesis 1 literally.[5] The leaders of the Reformation (c. 1517–1700) were unanimous in rejecting allegorization and in returning to a literal, grammatical–historical interpretation. Orthodox Jews also appear to have been unanimous in holding to a literal interpretation.[6] Incidentally, medieval theologians dealt mainly with the Vulgate, a Latin translation of the Bible, whereas the Reformers were able to study the Bible in the original languages. As mentioned already, Augustine himself had no knowledge of Hebrew.

It was only after secular scientists began developing their ideas of vast ages and evolution in the eighteenth and nineteenth centuries that Christians began to interpret Genesis 1–11 in terms of those ideas. Before then, long ages were not even thought of by conservative exegetes. This is strong evidence that those ideas *do not come from within* the Bible. They are alien ideas imported *into* the Bible.

It may be objected that similar things can be said of heliocentrism (the belief that the earth and other planets revolve around the sun). However, the geocentrism/heliocentrism debate is fundamentally different from both the young-earth/old-earth and the creation/evolution debates. Christians believed in a six-day special creation because they perceived that this is what the Bible teaches. But the primary reason for belief in geocentrism was not the teaching of the Bible. It was the fact that the sun and planets *appear* to revolve around the earth, and that the prevailing 'scientific' view at that time (established by a second-century Alexandrian Greek, Claudius Ptolemy) was geocentric. It can be shown quite easily that the Bible does not specify whether the solar system is geocentric or heliocentric, whereas it *does* specify the timescale of creation.

Responses to long-age and evolution theories

How did Christians respond to the challenge of long-age theories of geology, and then the theory of evolution? An early response was that of the 'scriptural geologists'. These people were forgotten for many years, but have been rediscovered recently by T. Mortenson.[7] One example is George Young (1777–1848), who was an ordained minister, but also an extremely competent geologist. They defended the historicity of Genesis 1–11, and argued that 'Flood geology' explains the observations of geology much better than the secular ideas of slow, gradual change. According to Flood geology, the whole surface of the planet was reshaped rapidly and catastrophically by the global Flood of Noah's day. Together with volcanic and tectonic activity on a huge scale, vastly exceeding anything that occurs now, it was responsible for most present-day geological features. Most fossils are the remains of organisms buried during and after the Flood. It is a popular misconception that 'Flood geology' was first thought of by young-earth creationists in the twentieth century; the truth is very different. Many early Christians, including Tertullian (c.155–230) and Augustine (354–430) believed that fossils are the remains of organisms buried in Noah's Flood. Later examples are Niels Steensen (1638–1686, also known as Nicolas Steno, the pioneer of modern geology) and John Woodward (1665–1722).[8]

There has always been a remnant who continued to believe that the Bible means what it says in Genesis 1–11. However, the majority of Christian leaders sought to harmonize the Bible with long-age theories of geology, and then later with the theory of evolution. William Buckland (1784–1856) is a prominent early example. He was an Anglican clergyman, and was the leading geologist in England in the 1820s. Various ways of adding millions of years to the Bible were invented. By adopting this approach, conservative Christians were trying to preserve Scripture; but in effect, I believe, they were trusting man's word rather than God's Word, and were placing science in authority over Scripture. Two main views came to be held: *concordism* and *discordism*. Concordism tries to preserve Genesis as history and reinterprets certain passages. It accepts the secular timeframe, and sometimes the theory of evolution also. Discordism regards Genesis as non-historical, and tends towards full-blown theistic evolution.

The most widespread concordist views are the 'gap theory' and the 'day-age theory'. The gap theory proposes that the fossils and rock layers are the remains of a *previous* creation which was destroyed by a great flood. These events are inserted into a supposed 'gap' between the first two verses of the Bible. The rest of the chapter is said to describe a *reconstruction* of the world in six days. The day-age theory proposes that the 'days' of creation were really long periods of time, each one lasting millions or billions of years.

As for discordism, there is only one main view in this camp if one wants to maintain any semblance of conservative Christianity. This is the 'literary framework theory'. It has recently become popular among evangelical academics who see the futility of the gap and day-age theories. Essentially, it views the creation account as figurative, thus leaving one free to accept theistic evolution—or virtually anything one fancies. If this theory is true, however, it is strange that the Reformers decisively rejected this kind of interpretation, and that no one thought of this particular version until 1924, when it was pioneered by Arie Noordtzij. (As described earlier, three of the Early Church Fathers and some medieval theologians had advocated figurative interpretations in the past; but it was Noordtzij who established the modern theory.) But as Sarfati comments, 'Actually, it's not so strange, because the leading framework exponents, Meredith Kline and Henri Blocher, admitted that their rationale for a bizarre, novel interpretation was a desperation to fit the Bible into the alleged "facts" of science.'[9] I will describe these old-earth theories in greater detail later.

As mentioned earlier, non-evangelical Hebrew scholars do not believe in the inerrancy of Scripture; so they are not worried about trying to harmonize the Bible with secular science. They are free to concentrate on the actual meaning of the Hebrew. As Hebrew scholars, they have no doubt whatsoever that the author of Genesis intended his readers to understand that creation took place in six literal days a few thousand years ago, and that Noah's Flood was worldwide.

What about the present-day resurgence of biblical creationism? The catalyst for this revival was the publication of *The Genesis Flood* by Whitcomb and Morris in 1961.[10] In this book the authors took an uncompromising stand on the authority and supremacy of Scripture, and the historicity of Genesis 1–11. They returned to the historic belief that God created the heavens and the earth in six days a few thousand years ago, and that Noah's Flood was worldwide. Their position was that of the 'scriptural geologists' of the early nineteenth century, all the Reformers, and nearly all the Early Church Fathers. This movement is now growing rapidly worldwide, and includes thousands of scientists and other specialists, many of whom are very highly qualified. A substantial number of them are university professors.

Biblical creationists deal with exactly the same *facts* as their secular counterparts; but they use a *biblical interpretive framework*, instead of a *naturalistic* framework. Many different fields of study are involved, and there are biblical creationists working in all of them. They include, for example, theology, Hebrew, cosmology, astronomy, physics, geology, palaeontology, zoology, botany, molecular biology, genetics, biochemistry, anthropology, archaeology and history. The secular humanist establishment has reacted to all this with fury and contempt; but I believe this is actually a good sign. It shows that Satan is worried! We are involved in spiritual warfare, and if we expose Satan's lies, this is the kind of reaction we should expect.

Roots and fruits

What, then, are the origins and consequences of the secular view of origins? The idea of evolution is actually very old. The pagan Greeks, for example, wrote about it some 2700 years ago. They did not use modern scientific language, of course, but they had no difficulty in expressing the idea that living things developed over vast periods of time. Clearly it is nonsense to say, as some do, that because 'the Bible is not a science textbook', it had to use figurative language to express the idea. If the Greeks were able to use ordinary language to describe long ages and evolution, I am sure God could have managed it!

As for the modern ideas of vast ages and evolution, their roots lie in the deism and atheism of the Enlightenment, or 'Age of Reason', in the seventeenth and eighteenth centuries. (The same can be said of liberal theology.) The god of the deist is not the God of Christianity. He is a remote being who started the universe, but left it to run itself, operating according to natural laws. The deist does not believe in divine revelation, and does not believe that the Bible is the word of God. Various theories were put forward over the course of time, resulting eventually in the full-blown uniformitarian geology of Charles Lyell (1797–1875) and then the theory of evolution of Charles Darwin (1809–1882). Lyell was a deist, and wrote that his intention was to 'liberate science from Moses'. Darwin was probably a deist or an agnostic; but he set out to craft a materialistic theory. He was much influenced by Charles Lyell and by his grandfather, Erasmus Darwin (1731–1802), who was an anti-Christian deist and evolutionist. Charles Lyell, in turn, was greatly influenced by the uniformitarian geology of the deist James Hutton (1726–1797). Lyell's theory was a radical uniformitarianism in which he insisted that only present-day processes at present-day rates of intensity and magnitude should be used to interpret the rock record.[11] Thus the roots of these ideas (of vast ages and evolution) are clearly anti-biblical and anti-Christian.

What about the fruit of these ideas? The list of evil fruit seems almost endless. Whole nations and societies have been affected for evil. Countless millions of individual people have been affected for evil. It has caused untold misery and suffering. Science itself has been corrupted and led down a dead-end path. The theory of evolution (with the billions of years which it requires) is *the* foundational belief of secular humanism. It enables humanists to deny the existence of God and their accountability to him. It means that they create their own standard of morality, and they do 'what is right in their own eyes' (see Judges 21:25). Nations and societies which adopt this philosophy see a breakdown of family life, broken homes, sexual immorality, lack of respect for the sanctity of human life (including that of the unborn child), increasing crime, etc. This is seen in the UK already, and is the logical outcome of ignoring the clear evidence of God's 'eternal power and deity' in the creation, of 'suppressing the truth', of 'exchanging the truth of God for the lie', and of 'worshipping and serving the creature rather than the Creator' (Romans 1:18–32). The theory of evolution is foundational also to the atheistic doctrines of Marxism and Nazism, and has produced the same results along with the cold-blooded murder of millions. It is the basis of the most appalling eugenics (the science of producing fine offspring) and racism of various kinds, involving the ruthless elimination of those regarded as inferior.

Such are the logical outcomes of the whole concept of evolution, and of the rejection of the biblical account of creation. That account teaches that all humans are created in God's image, and are of one race, being descended from one couple, Adam and Eve. And they were created male and female—the foundation of the Bible's teaching on sex and marriage. And it was only after Adam and Eve had disobeyed God that pain, suffering and death entered the world. The early chapters of Genesis are foundational to Christian doctrine, and the theory of evolution deliberately attacks those foundations.

The theory of evolution is directly or indirectly responsible for the loss of faith or lack of faith of millions. Witness the millions of atheists in countries which used to be 'Christian', but have been or are dominated by communism or secular humanism. And there are countless stories of individuals who were brought up in Christian homes, but lost their faith through evolutionary teaching. I will give just two examples. David Duke is the leader of several racist groups in America, including the Ku Klux Klan and the American Nazi party. He was brought up in a Christian home, his father being a Sunday school teacher. When race became an area of serious study for Duke, he no longer relied upon the Bible, but instead relied on science, specifically Darwinism. In his autobiography, he has detailed how he studied evolutionary theory in detail and rejected Genesis and creationism, especially the teaching that all people are descended from Adam.[12]

My second example is Charles Templeton, who was once an evangelist more famous than Billy Graham. However, he became convinced that the theory of evolution is true, and as a result, he lost his faith completely. This is what he wrote:

> The grim and inescapable reality is that all life is predicated on death. Every carnivorous creature must kill and devour another creature. It has no option. How could a loving and omnipotent God create such horrors? ... Surely it would not be beyond the competence of an omniscient deity to create an animal world that could be sustained and perpetuated without suffering and death.[13]

Note that this statement applies not only to the theory of evolution, but also to all the 'old-earth' theories which try to reconcile the biblical account of creation with 'millions of years'.

Another fruit of the ideas of vast ages and evolution is the slide into liberal theology. If you disbelieve one part of the Bible, you are more liable to disbelieve other parts. Princeton Theological Seminary, where Charles Templeton studied, is a good example. It started as a thoroughly evangelical, Bible-believing college. But then Hodge (1797–1878) put one foot on the top of the slippery slope when he chose to believe 'science' on one point of creation rather than the plain meaning of Scripture. B. B. Warfield (1851–1921) went one step further when he accepted the theory of evolution. Subsequent generations went even further, and Princeton is now thoroughly liberal. This kind of teaching (that the Bible can be harmonized with the secular view of origins) is now routine in most evangelical theological colleges in the West—and it is being exported to our brothers and sisters in the developing world.

I suggest that the anti-Christian origin and evil fruit of these theories indicate very clearly that they are a satanic deception. Satan is the father of lies, and is constantly seeking to deceive the world, and to corrupt and destroy the church. Another sign of the true nature of these theories is the way in which secular scientists do all in their power to exclude biblical creationist teaching from education and the media, and to impose their own views. They claim that evolution is science, and that creation is religion; but actually, the theory of evolution is no more scientific than creationism. It is a materialistic faith or philosophy (I will say more about this later), and is the foundational belief of secular humanism. We should be attacking it, not compromising with it.

Notes

1. **J. Sarfati,** *Refuting Compromise* (Green Forest, AR: Master Books, 2004).

2. See **Robert Bradshaw's** in-depth study, 'Genesis, Creationism and the Early Church', Chapter 3: www.robibrad.demon.co.uk/Chapter3.htm, 13 August 2003.

3. **Fr. Rose's** papers were published posthumously in *Genesis, Creation and Early Man* (Platina, CA, 2000).

4. **Batten and Sarfati,** *15 Reasons*, pp. 18–19.

5. **J. Mook,** *The Early Church on Creation,* in *Answers*, Oct.–Dec. 2007, pp. 66–67.

6. **P. James-Griffiths,** creation.com/creation-days-and-orthodox-jewish-tradition

7. **T. Mortenson,** *The Great Turning Point* (Green Forest, AR: Master Books, 2004).

8. Ibid. pp. 25–26.

9. **Sarfati,** *Refuting Compromise*, p. 136.

10. **J. C. Whitcomb and H. M. Morris,** *The Genesis Flood* (Philadelphia: Presbyterian and Reformed Publishing Co., 1961).

11. **Mortenson,** *The Great Turning Point*, pp. 24–33.

12. **D. Duke,** *My Awakening: A Path to Racial Understanding* (Covington, LA: Free Speech Press, 1998), p. 256.

13. **C. Templeton,** *Farewell to God* (Toronto: McLelland and Stewart, 1996), pp. 197–199.

The Bible

This brings us to the issue of what the Bible says, and how it is meant to be understood. I have mentioned 'the plain meaning of Scripture', and I intend to show what I mean by this. But first I would like to point out one reason why it is important to understand that the creation account is real history, and is not figurative.

The lessons of the creation account are much more powerful and authoritative if these things really happened. If they did not actually happen in the manner described, the lessons are not backed up by the facts; so nothing is proved. It is the same with all history in the Bible. Christianity is a historical religion. God has revealed himself through mighty acts of power in history. If the resurrection is just a story, and did not actually happen, our faith is futile (1 Corinthians 15:17). If the Exodus account is just a story, it proves nothing. If it is just a story, why does the Bible point to it repeatedly as a demonstration of God's mighty, saving power? It is the same with predictive prophecy. *Genuine* predictive prophecy in the Bible proves that God is the only true God (Isaiah 41:21–23; 44:6–8; 46:9–10; 48:3–5). Pseudo-prophecy proves nothing, and pseudo-history likewise proves nothing.

So what does the Bible really teach about creation? This section owes much to Batten and Sarfati's booklet, *15 Reasons to Take Genesis as History*. I acknowledge my indebtedness to it, and I recommend it to you as a more detailed and scholarly treatment of the subject. An even more detailed treatment is Sarfati's 400-page book, *Refuting Compromise*.

Jesus' attitude to Scripture

The first point to make is that as Christians, we should follow Jesus' example in his attitude to the Old Testament Scriptures. He regarded them as God's word—that is, spoken by God or inspired by the Holy Spirit, although written by the hands of men. Even the smallest letter or stroke was inspired. He treated them as completely authoritative. He rebuked people for not believing them, especially the books of Moses, the first of which is the book of Genesis (John 5:45–47). Notice that his attitude was exactly the same both before and after his resurrection (Luke 24:25–27, 44–45). When he referred to Genesis 2:24, for example, he endorsed the divine authorship of Scripture in a most remarkable way:

> Perhaps the crowning example of his attitude is to be found in Matthew 19:4–5. It is all the more impressive because it is so natural. Jesus is quoting the words of Genesis 2:24, in itself a comment passed by the author of Genesis, and he ascribes them to God himself. 'Have you not read that *he who made them* … *said*, "For this reason a man shall leave his father and mother and be joined to his wife"?' Clearly Jesus regarded this statement of the author of Genesis as nothing less than spoken by God himself, even though the Genesis account does not directly attribute it to the Almighty. A word of Scripture was a word of God.[1]

Batten and Sarfati remark:

> A proper hermeneutic (interpretive method) that is consistent with Jesus' attitude involves *exegesis*, or reading *out of* Scripture the message the writer was teaching—not *eisegesis*, or reading things *into* Scripture. That is, an honest reading of Scripture entails finding out what God is saying, not what the reader can make it say that would make it palatable or conform to current popular opinion.[2]

Jesus and creation

The second point is that Jesus clearly regarded the account of Adam and Eve's creation as factual, as well as the Flood. He affirmed many people and events of the past that sceptics deny ever existed or happened: Adam and Eve (Matthew 19:3–6; Mark 10:2–9), Abel (Luke 11:51), Noah and the Flood (Matthew 24:37–39; Luke 17:26–27), Abraham (John 8:56–58), Sodom and Gomorrah (Matthew 10:15; 11:23–24), Daniel (Matthew 24:15), Jonah and the great sea creature (Matthew 12:39–41).

Jesus indicated also that he did not understand world history in terms of billions of years with man arriving very recently. Rather, he placed man at the *beginning* of creation:

- 'But from the beginning of the creation, God "made them male and female"' (Mark 10:6);
- '... the blood of all the prophets which was shed from the foundation of the world ... from the blood of Abel to the blood of Zechariah ...' (Luke 11:50–51).

'The creation' includes *time*, as well as matter/energy and space. Therefore when Jesus said 'the beginning of the creation', he meant the beginning of time, as well as the beginning of matter/energy and space. According to theistic evolution and all other 'old-earth' creation theories, man appeared at the *end* of billions of years of creation.

What kind of literature?

The third point is that Genesis was written as *history*. Hebrew literature used special grammatical structures for consecutive historical narrative, and Genesis 1–11 has those structures. It has the same form as that of Genesis 12–50 and most of Exodus, Joshua, Judges, etc. The grammatical structure is that of consecutive narrative prose, *not poetry*, and in the context of Genesis and the rest of the Bible, it is clearly *historical* narrative. Sarfati (who is a Jewish Christian) goes into the Hebrew, but you will need to consult his books for the details. I have quoted Professor James Barr on the subject already. He stated flatly that as far as he knew, no professor of Hebrew at any major university doubts that the author of Genesis 1–11 intended his readers to understand that there was a literal six-day creation a few thousand years ago, and a global Flood. Evangelical Hebrew scholars such as Professor Robert McCabe, Professor Steven Boyd and Dr Ting Wang agree that this is the clear, unambiguous meaning of the Hebrew text. Professor Edward J. Young, an eminent evangelical Hebrew scholar, is another who has stressed that the grammatical structure of Genesis 1 is that of narrative prose, *not poetry*.

Incidentally, one of the differences between poetry and historical narrative in the Old Testament is the use of different verb forms. A project was undertaken quite recently in which a statistical analysis of verb forms in the Old Testament was conducted by computer. It showed overwhelmingly that the verb forms used in Genesis 1–11 are characteristic of historical narrative, *not* poetry.[3] The events described in Genesis 1–11 are extraordinary, and the description of creation in Genesis 1 is beautiful, majestic, structured and unique; *but that does not make the account symbolical.* The grammatical structure and context indicate very clearly that it is consecutive, historical narrative.

It is true that the first chapter of Genesis is very special literature, and its style is somewhat different from that of the following chapters. But that, I suggest, is because of its very special subject matter, and its very special origin. The only eyewitness of creation was God himself. If the account is factual history, it must have been received by direct revelation from God. The beautiful structure, symmetry and inbuilt mathematics are there quite simply because that is the way God chose to create the world and universe, and that is the way he chose to reveal it. His method of creation displayed his rationality, orderliness, perfection and omnipotence—and there are other reasons also, which I describe later. It is the complete antithesis of macro-evolution (the molecules-to-man kind of evolution), which is a slow, nasty, messy, haphazard, inefficient, wasteful, brutal, hypothetical process, sprawling over millions of years, and producing an imperfect world.

The days of creation
The fourth point is that the 'days' of creation are identified very clearly, in four different ways, as literal days. The Hebrew word *yom* usually means a literal, twenty-four-hour day, or day as opposed to night; but it does have other meanings. However, it is always obvious from the context which meaning is intended. The only days in the Bible about which people disagree are the days of creation and the reason for this disagreement is not that the Bible is unclear. On the contrary, the Bible is very clear indeed. Rather, the reasons for this disagreement are *external*—namely the desire to conform the Bible to 'science', or simply an unwillingness to believe that God would or could have created the universe in six literal days.

To start with, God stated unambiguously that he created the heavens and the earth in six days, and he wrote it down on a tablet of stone (Exodus 20:11; 31:17–18). The *context* of this statement is that of an ordinary seven-day week.

The context indicates very clearly indeed, therefore, that these days of creation were *literal* twenty-four-hour days. And when we look at the creation account itself in Genesis 1, we see that the days are clearly identified *in three different ways* as literal days. First, when 'day' in the Old Testament is associated with a number, cardinal or ordinal, it *always* means a literal day. Second, when 'day' in the Old Testament is associated with evening or morning, it *always* means a literal day. Third, right at the beginning of Genesis 1, in verses 3–5, the meaning of 'day' is defined for us in a very specific way. It is given two meanings: day as opposed to night; and a full twenty-four-hour period of darkness and light. For a fuller exposition of this point, see *Refuting Compromise*.4

Scripture interprets Scripture

The fifth point is the hermeneutical principle that Scripture interprets Scripture. Both the Old Testament and the New Testament take Genesis 1–11 as *history*. I have mentioned Exodus 20:11 and 31:17–18 already. In 1 Chronicles 1 we find a summary of the genealogical data from Adam onwards in Genesis, and many other Old Testament passages affirm the events of Genesis as being historical (real events in time and space). In the New Testament, there are over 100 quotations from or allusions to Genesis 1–11, none of which hints at Genesis being anything other than history. Jesus' genealogy (Luke 3) goes back to Adam, 'the son of God'—not the son of a hominid! To those who say that the early names are mere metaphors, we ask: As we trace the lineage back, where do the people stop being real and become metaphors? Hebrews 11 lists heroes of the faith, starting with Abel, Enoch and Noah, without the tiniest hint that they are less historical than the others. Jesus and Peter refer to the Flood, using a special word for the global cataclysm of Genesis, *kataklusmos* (Matt. 24:38–39; Luke 17:27; 2 Peter 2:5). The verbal form, *katakluzo*, is used in 2 Peter 3:6. These words are not used for ordinary floods, as in Luke 6:48. In his teaching on the roles of men and women, Paul cites the order of creation of Adam and Eve, as well as the fact that Eve was deceived while Adam sinned anyway (1 Timothy 2:13–14). What kind of teaching is this, if the first true humans evolved from a population of hominids?

Death and suffering

The sixth point is that the biblical account of creation is necessary to explain death and suffering—not only in the human race (see below), but also in nature as a whole. God's creation is amazing and beautiful; but there is also much violence, suffering, disease and death. There are natural disasters. The balance of nature depends on predators killing and devouring their prey. It depends on the survival of the fittest, 'Nature, red in tooth and claw', as Tennyson wrote. Animals have diseases, and they suffer fear and pain, especially the more intelligent ones. As for *fossil* animals, all are silent witnesses to death; many also show signs of violence, and some show signs of disease, such as cancer. If they represent millions of years of life on earth, it means that there were millions of years of violence, suffering, disease and death *before* Adam and Eve disobeyed God. Note that these fossils include human beings who are believed by old-earthers to be Adam and Eve's ancestors. *Homo sapiens* fossils with evidence of intelligent cultural activity have been 'dated' at 160,000 years old.[5] It means also that *God's method of creation* was a process of millions of years of wasteful, bloody, and totally unnecessary carnage and suffering. It was unnecessary, because he is omnipotent and could easily have created a perfect world and universe in six days (or fewer) without any kind of suffering or death.

Most people can see that a method of creation which entails millions of years of unnecessary suffering is incompatible with belief in an omnipotent and loving God. They deduce correctly that a god who chooses to use such a method must be both cruel and incompetent. It certainly does not inspire awe and wonder in such people. Very often it destroys what little faith they have. It destroyed Charles Templeton's faith. And when someone asked David Attenborough why he does not see God's hand in the wonders of creation, this was the kind of reason he gave.

What does the Bible say? The crystal clear answer is that God's original creation was flawless—absolutely perfect—and that evil, both moral and physical, came into the world *as a consequence of Adam and Eve's disobedience*. We are told six times in Genesis 1 that God saw that his creation was 'good', and the seventh time he saw that it was 'very good'. Seven is the perfect number, and it emphasizes the absolute perfection of God's 'very good' creation. God is omnipotent, omniscient and absolutely good. The presence in God's original creation of *any* kind of evil, moral or physical, is absolutely denied.

The Bible tells us that human death is the consequence of Adam and Eve's disobedience. It is made perfectly clear that this means physical death, as well as spiritual death (Genesis 2:15–3:24; Romans 5:12–21; 1 Corinthians 15:12–58). 'The last enemy that will be destroyed is death' (1 Corinthians 15:26; cf. Isaiah 25:7–8; Revelation 21:4). But there were other consequences also, both to the human race and to the whole creation. A curse was placed upon creation, and this is referred to in Genesis 3:14–24, Romans 8:18–25 and Revelation 21:4; 22:3. The whole creation has been 'subjected to futility', is in 'the bondage of corruption' or 'decay', and is 'groaning' because of this curse.

One consequence of this curse was animal carnivory (carnivorous behaviour), suffering and death. I have dealt with this subject in detail in an article published in the *Journal of Creation* (*TJ*);[6] but I can mention only a few points here. In Genesis 1:29–30; 9:3 and Isaiah 11:6–9; 65:17–25 there are very clear indications that in the original, perfect creation men and animals were herbivorous—they ate vegetable matter only. They were not carnivorous. The Isaiah passages picture conditions in the new creation which is yet to come; but they hint very strongly that this will be a return, in some sense, to conditions as they were before the Fall (see also Matthew 19:28; Acts 3:21; Romans 8:19–22).[7] They indicate very clearly that there is something *wrong* about animal carnivory. They indicate also that man's religious condition is responsible for this state of things—human sin and evil in nature are interconnected in a relation of cause and effect.[8] These things are true whether the passages are taken literally or metaphorically. The message is conveyed not only by the overall picture, but also by the meaning of the Hebrew words employed:

> Actually, these passages indicate very specifically that carnivorous activity is an
> evil—that is, a physical rather than a moral evil. The Hebrew word translated 'hurt'
> in the KJV of Isaiah 11:9 and 65:25 is *raa*. Elsewhere in the Old Testament, the most
> frequent translation of this word is 'do evil.' Other translations include 'afflict' and

'do wickedly.' It is related to *ra*, the usual word for 'evil' in the Old Testament—and that includes both moral and physical evil. As for the word translated 'destroy' in the KJV of Isaiah 11:9 and 65:25 (*shachath*), the core meaning is 'mar' or 'corrupt.' No wonder carnivorous activity has no place in the new creation![9]

This means that carnivorous activity is a physical 'evil', and is therefore part of the curse—it was not present in the original, perfect creation. This is incompatible with all old-earth views, because the fossils show clear evidence of carnivory on a massive scale. These animals experienced pain, fear, disease, violence, carnivory and death in just the same way as animals do today. And the same is true of the *human* fossils, which old-earth creationists believe pre-dated Adam and Eve (if they believe that Adam and Eve were real people).

What about animal death? The Bible does not mention *animal* death specifically in this context, and there are obvious 'difficulties' with the belief that there was no animal death in the original creation. I will show later that the difficulties are more apparent than real; but what is the biblical evidence in favour of this belief? First, as I have shown, the Bible teaches that the original creation was perfect, and animals did not kill each other. Death caused by injury, disease or the decrepitude of old age can hardly be described as 'very good' either. Second, we are told that death is 'the last enemy', and will be banished from the new creation. Perhaps this refers only to human death, but it seems more likely that *all* death is meant. Third, when man was cursed, the whole creation was cursed as well; so it is logical that the animal world suffered the same curse of death. Fourth, in animal sacrifices, animal death was used to symbolize Jesus' death on the cross and the punishment of human sin. Fifth, Romans 8:21 describes the cursed creation as being in 'the bondage of corruption' or 'decay'. Animal death is a form of corruption or decay. Sixth, animal death can cause unhappiness and feelings of bereavement, especially when the animal has been a much-loved pet. In fact, it seems that in the case of many animals, especially intelligent ones like elephants, the death of one of their own kind can cause grief and distress to the animals themselves. Is it likely that something which causes unhappiness had a place in Paradise? Also, feelings of utter revulsion can be caused by the sight of a predator killing and ripping apart its prey, or by the stench of a rotting carcase. Is it likely that these things were part of Paradise—a perfect, very good creation?

Genesis is foundational

The seventh point is that the history of Genesis is foundational to the gospel. In fact, every major Christian doctrine is rooted in the historical facts of Genesis, directly or indirectly. And it is important that these historical facts are *real*, in just the same way that it is important that the bodily resurrection of Jesus and other historical events in the Bible are real. Romans 5:12–17, with 1 Corinthians 15:20–22; 45–49, grounds the meaning of Jesus' bodily death and resurrection in the real history of Genesis. A real man, Adam, brought bodily death ('to dust you shall return', Genesis 3:19) and corruption into God's 'very good' world by his sin. Likewise, a real man, the God-Man from heaven, came to undo the work of the first man, the federal head of the human race. Just as one man brought death to all who are in him, so one perfect man brings life to all who are in him.[10]

The early chapters of Genesis give us vital information about God, about us and our relationship with him, about the Fall and its consequences, and about the world and universe. They are the basis of Christian teaching about, for example, the Sabbath, the sanctity of human life, the unity of the human race, man's stewardship of creation, the reason for moral and physical evil in the world, sex and marriage. The theory of evolution attacks these foundations, and the consequences are obvious—not only in society, but also in the church. Acceptance of these ideas involves denial of the clear teaching of Scripture, and sooner or later leads to other kinds of compromise. If we deny the truth of Scripture on one point, what is there to stop us denying it on other points?

The fact that the biblical account of creation is foundational to the gospel is relevant to the task of mission. When the gospel is taken to people who have no knowledge of Christianity or Judaism, it is necessary to start at the beginning before jumping in with the gospel. The foundations need to be laid first. This was Paul's method with the pagan Greeks in Athens. If the missionary does not believe that the early chapters of Genesis are real history, a difficult task is made even more difficult. The 'literary framework' theory, for example, is useless in such a situation. The *real history* of Genesis makes sense to every kind of person in every culture. This is true of both the developing world and the secular West. Most people do not know who the Christian God is, who we are, where we came from, and why we are here. They do not know the meaning of sin and death. They need to understand these things before they can understand the gospel. God has given us the answers to these questions in the early chapters of Genesis; but many in the church have scrapped Genesis as real history! The awful truth is that *the church itself* has contributed to the present situation by helping to destroy the very foundations of the gospel. It has done so by capitulating to secular science's version of history, rather than believing and teaching God's Word.

The creation was finished

The eighth point is that the theory of evolution is incompatible with Genesis 2:1–2. We are told that God *finished* his work of creation on the sixth day, and then he rested from his work of creation. Furthermore, the Bible teaches that since the Fall, the creation has been under a curse, and is now *decaying* (Genesis 3:14–24; Romans 8:18–25). This is totally incompatible with theistic evolution. According to that theory, creation through evolution never stopped—it is still going on today. Furthermore, the facts of science support the biblical teaching, not the evolutionary teaching. When we look around us, we see a world and universe which are *running down*. This is true of living things, as well as of the inanimate universe. Two of the most fundamental laws of physics are the first and second laws of thermodynamics. The first law supports the biblical teaching that God *finished* his work of creation. The second law supports the biblical teaching that the creation is decaying, or running down.

They are without excuse

The ninth point is that the theory of evolution is incompatible with Romans 1:20 and 2 Peter 3:3–7. In Romans we are told that since the creation of the world, God's power and divine nature can be clearly seen in creation; so people are without excuse. If the theory of evolution were true, people *would* have an excuse for not believing in God. They would have good reason to say that there is no need to believe in God, because evolution is a blind, cruel, natural process, operating by chance alone. The whole point of the theory of evolution, in the minds of those who invented it, is that it dispenses with the need for God. It is a *natural* process which requires no supernatural interference. The term 'theistic evolution' is really an oxymoron. I suspect that most secular scientists regard the idea as a joke, secretly if not openly.

From 2 Peter 3:3–7 we see that we should know about creation by God's word (as in Romans 1:20), and we should know about the global Flood. Not only do we have the physical evidence of the Flood preserved in the rocks, but also we have mankind's collective memory of it preserved in many Flood legends all over the world.

Note that the Bible presents Creation and the Flood as being so obvious that anyone who denies their reality is wilfully ignorant and worthy of God's judgment (Romans 1:18–32 and 2 Peter 3:3–7). If 'evolution' explains our origins such that God's actions are invisible, and there is no evidence for the Flood (modern historical geology), then why does God hold unbelievers culpable?[11]

Divine fiat

The tenth point is that taking Genesis as history is consistent with other divine fiat acts in history. 'Fiat' means a decree or command. Genesis tells us that God spoke things into existence. God speaks, and things happen. As it says in Psalm 33:9, 'He spoke, and it was done; he commanded, and it stood fast.'

Most of Jesus' (God the Son's) miracles were of this nature. He spoke, and it happened—immediately. This included obviously creative acts, like the turning of water into wine, and the multiplication of the loaves and fish. But almost all his miracles were creative in some way. In the case of the centurion's servant he healed by word of command without even seeing the servant. When he spoke to the wind and waves they obeyed him instantly.

Some Christians say that they find the thought of creation over millions of years more impressive and awe-inspiring than the thought of creation in six days. I wonder if they really understand what that means? In the former case, it means that God the Son (Colossians 1:16) created an *imperfect* world and universe by means of a slow, cruel, inefficient, wasteful process which involved the suffering and death of billions of creatures. The alternative is that he spoke a *perfect* world and universe into existence over a period of six days. Of course, he could have done it in an instant; but by doing it in a certain order over a period of six days, he was teaching certain lessons, as I will show later.

A coherent worldview and eschatology

The eleventh point is that the history of Genesis is necessary for a coherent biblical worldview and eschatology (study of the last things). For example, one aspect of the biblical worldview is that man and this world are of central, supreme importance in creation. Man was made in the image of God and was placed in this world, and God became man in this world (Genesis 1:27–28; John 1:1–3, 14). This is in complete harmony with the history of Genesis 1. According to that account, man has been in the world from the *beginning* of creation (Genesis 1:1–31; Mark 10:6; Luke 11:50–51; Romans 1:20, etc.), and the world was created *before* the rest of the universe (Genesis 1:2, 14–19). Christians who believe in the secular 'big-bang' hypothesis have to believe that man's existence is a mere blip at the very *end* of billions of years of creation (a clear contradiction of Jesus' words in Mark 10:6 and Luke 11:50–51, and of Romans 1:20 etc.), and that there is nothing special about this world's position in time and space.

As for eschatology, this involves another aspect of the biblical worldview. We are told that God will purge the universe by fire and create new heavens and a new earth (2 Peter 3:7–13). But why should he do this if the present world and universe are much the same as they were before the Fall, as believed by old-earthers? The problem with the present creation is not simply that man has misused and spoiled the world. Romans 8:18–25, Colossians 1:20 and 2 Peter 3:7–13 indicate that God subjected the entire creation to corruption or decay after man rebelled against him. The present creation is radically different from the original 'very good' creation, and will be radically transformed when Jesus returns.

The Bible indicates that the creation will be restored to the state (or something resembling the state) that it enjoyed before the Fall. In particular, there will be no decay, and no violence, carnivory, suffering and death—a truly radical transformation. See Isaiah 11:6–9; 25:7–8; 65:17–25; Acts 3:21; Romans 8:18–

25; 1 Corinthians 15:12–58; 2 Peter 3:3–13; Revelation 21:1–4; 22:3. This teaching is wrecked by the various old-earth theories, because all such theories say that these physical evils existed long before the Fall.

Jesus said that when he returns to judge the world, it will be as in the days of Noah, when 'the flood came and destroyed them all' (Luke 17:26–27). Peter also likened the coming destruction of the universe by fire with the destruction of the world by Noah's Flood. This makes sense only if the Flood was worldwide and truly catastrophic. He prophesied that scoffers would come in the last days who would be wilfully ignorant of the creation of heaven and earth by God's word, and its subsequent destruction by the Flood. They would say that 'all things continue as they were from the beginning of creation' (2 Peter 3:3–13). This is a good description of today's uniformitarian paradigm, with its theory of evolution and its denial of the global Flood.

Disconnected from the real world
The twelfth point is that disbelieving the history of Genesis disconnects the Bible from the real world. This was exactly the case with the evangelical leader with whom I debated: he described the biblical teaching about creation as 'the internal witness of Scripture'. In the average person's mind, religion which is disconnected from the real world is simply irrelevant. It is nothing more than a matter of faith or opinion. He or she reasons, very sensibly, that if we disbelieve what the Bible says about creation, why should we believe anything else it says? If we cannot believe the Bible on matters of history and science, which concern the real world of time and space, why should we believe what it says about God (cf. John 3:12)?

But of course, Christianity is not disconnected from the real world of time and space. It is rooted in real history. It is tied up with God's activity in the real world— the real history of creation, the Flood, the Exodus, the resurrection of Jesus and many other events. Again and again the Bible points to God's mighty acts of power in history. It is essential to the truth of Christianity that these historical events are real.

The trouble with allowing 'science' to dictate our understanding of Genesis is that there is no good reason why it should not dictate our understanding of other parts of the Bible also. The many miraculous signs around the time of the Exodus do not accord with 'modern scientific knowledge'; so they ought to be jettisoned too. Modern science tells us that people do not rise from the dead; so the resurrection of Jesus ought to be jettisoned as well. Why should we believe the eyewitness accounts of those who saw the risen Jesus when we do not believe the eyewitness account of creation which was given by God himself? Jesus indicated very clearly that the words of the creation account are the words of God (Matthew 19:4–5). Not only did God reveal that he created the universe in six literal days, as explained above, but also he confirmed it to Moses on Mount Sinai.

One argument employed by old-earthers is that 'the Bible is not a science textbook'. However, this is irrelevant. A factual historical account does not need to be written in scientific language. As I have pointed out already, if God had created the world and universe by evolution over a long period of time, it would have been very easy to say so in non-scientific language—just as the Greeks did 2700 years ago.

Another argument is that 'the creation account is about *why* God created, not *how* he created'. This sounds impressive, but it is wrong! As indicated already, the Hebrew grammatical structure of the account itself, the rest of the Old Testament, the New Testament and Jesus himself make it perfectly clear that the creation account is *historical narrative*, and is therefore about the 'how' as well as the 'why'.

Another favourite argument is that biblical creationists are invoking a 'god of the gaps'. That is, we are using God to fill the gaps in our scientific knowledge—gaps which are growing smaller and smaller. However, this argument effectively cedes all authority to 'science', and implies that the Bible cannot speak with authority in this area. But our God is the God of the Bible, not a god of the gaps. Our position is that if there is a conflict between the clear teaching of Scripture and the majority opinion of scientists, it is the scientists who are wrong, not the Bible. In any case, the gaps are real, and they are getting bigger, not smaller! The more we learn about God's amazing creation, the more it is apparent that naturalism cannot account for it. Note, however, that biblical creationists do not say merely that the evidence cannot be explained naturalistically (a negative statement). They say also that the evidence *clearly points to intelligent design and special creation* (a positive statement). Or, as Romans 1:20 puts it, 'the things that are made' point to God's 'eternal power and Godhead' so clearly that we are 'without excuse'. The 'god of the gaps' argument completely fails to understand and appreciate the two-pronged nature of the intelligent-design argument.

These arguments against biblical creationism are simply ways of denying the account's historicity, so that it can be reconciled with 'science'.

Grammatical–historical interpretation

Finally, it is important to make it clear that although biblical creationists believe in the inerrancy and supreme authority of Scripture, it does not mean that we are wooden literalists. Here is another quotation from *15 Reasons*:

> Please note that belief in inerrancy does not mean wooden literalism (a common straw-man argument). Inerrantists such as us apply the standard, orthodox, grammatical-historical hermeneutic [method of interpretation], which recognizes the various forms of writing such as metaphor, hyperbole, etc.[12] In other words, we take as literal history those passages which were clearly intended to be taken as such (including Gen. 1–11).[13]

Notes

1. **M. Green,** *The Authority of Scripture* (London: Falcon, 1963), p. 11.
2. **Batten and Sarfati,** *15 Reasons*, p. 4.
3. **D. DeYoung,** *Thousands … Not Billions* (Green Forest, AR: Master Books, 2005), pp. 158–170.
4. **Sarfati,** *Refuting Compromise*, pp. 67–105.
5. **Batten and Sarfati,** *15 Reasons*, p. 11.
6. **R. J. M. Gurney,** 'The Carnivorous Nature and Suffering of Animals', in *Journal of Creation (TJ)*, **18**(3): 70–75, 2004.
7. **A. Motyer,** *The Prophecy of Isaiah* (Leicester: IVP, 1993), p. 124.
8. **N. M. de S. Cameron,** *Evolution and the Authority of the Bible* (Exeter: Paternoster Press, 1983), pp. 58–59.
9. **Gurney,** 'Carnivorous Nature and Suffering of Animals', p. 71.
10. **Sarfati,** *Refuting Compromise*, p. 14.
11. **Batten and Sarfati,** *15 Reasons*, p. 15.
12. A good summary is: **R. Grigg,** 'Should Genesis be Taken Literally?', in *Creation* 16(1): 38–41, 1993; creation.com/should-genesis-be-taken-literally.
13. **Batten and Sarfati,** *15 Reasons*, p. 5.

Old-earth theories

In this section I will take a very brief look at the main theories which attempt to reconcile the Bible with the theory of evolution, or with a billions-of-years timescale. Fuller critiques by biblical creationists can be found in books such as *Refuting Compromise*, by Jonathan Sarfati, and on creationist websites. The fact that these theories were not thought of until geologists began to advocate vast ages is a clear indication that they are being read *into* Scripture, not out of it. And the fact that there are so many old-earth theories is an indication of their inadequacy. Trying to squeeze evolution and billions of years into the biblical account of creation is like trying to fit a square peg into a round hole.

Different old-earth theories suffer from different weaknesses, but there is one fatal weakness which is common to all of them. All involve violence, bloodshed, disease, pain, suffering and death *before Adam and Eve disobeyed God.* Billions of creatures suffered and died. And, according to these theories, suffering and death were experienced not only by animals, but also by alleged pre-Adamite humans and/or 'hominids'. These features are clearly unbiblical, whatever proponents of the theories may say to justify them.

The gap theory
There are different versions of this theory. Basically, the classical theory proposes that the fossils and rock layers are the remains of a *previous* creation which was ruled over by Satan. After he fell, the earth was destroyed by a great flood, thus producing the fossils and rock layers. These events are inserted into a supposed 'gap' between the first two verses of Genesis 1. The second verse is required to say that the earth *became* (rather than 'was') formless and empty. The rest of the chapter describes a *reconstruction* of the world in six literal days. An influential book which promotes this theory is *Earth's Earliest Ages* by G. H. Pember, first published in 1884. Other versions of the gap theory have tried to overcome the shortcomings of the classical version, but all have serious problems.

This theory is so obviously unsatisfactory that most scholars have abandoned it. It has many flaws, both biblical and scientific. For example, Exodus 20:11 says, 'For in six days the LORD made the heavens and the earth, the sea, *and all that is in them* ...' Also, the Hebrew does not allow a gap between the first two verses, nor does it allow the meaning required in the second verse. Furthermore, the theory makes no sense geologically.

The day-age theory

This theory tries to uphold the historicity of the creation account, and its proponents try to show that the order of creation in Genesis 1 corresponds to the order of creation 'revealed' by science. The days of creation are considered to be long periods of time, each one lasting millions or billions of years. Most who subscribe to this view are 'progressive creationists'. They recognize the discontinuity of the fossil record, and propose that there were periods of great creative activity, separated by long periods of 'horizontal' diversification or 'micro-evolution'. An influential book which supports this theory is *The Christian View of Science and Scripture* by Bernard Ramm. The most prominent proponent today is Hugh Ross.

The first weakness of this theory is that the days of creation cannot be interpreted as long periods of time. This is recognized by non-evangelical Hebrew scholars, and also by gap theorists and literary framework theorists. 'With the Lord one day is as a thousand years, and a thousand years as one day' (2 Peter 3:8) is often cited. But this statement is a general truth, explaining that God is outside time. It is irrelevant to the meaning of 'day' in this context. That has to be determined on the basis of what the account says, how it says it, the context, and how the rest of the Bible understands it.

The second weakness is that it is impossible to reconcile the order of creation in Genesis with the order of creation 'revealed by science'. Davis Young, who was a Christian professor of geology, used to be a day-age proponent; but he gave up in despair when he finally realized that it is impossible to make the biblical order agree with the 'scientific' order. He now regards the biblical account as figurative.

The literary framework theory

This theory recognizes that the days of creation are meant to be understood as twenty-four-hour days, but it regards them and the whole account as figurative or symbolical. This leaves its proponents free to embrace the theory of evolution or any other theory. Most in this camp are theistic evolutionists. They accept the whole deistic/atheist concept of 'vertical' macro-evolution (the molecules-to-man kind of evolution), but they think that this was *God's* method of creation. An influential book which supports the literary framework theory is *In the Beginning* by Henri Blocher.

How do they justify this figurative understanding? They downplay or ignore the fact that the grammatical structure of the Hebrew is that of the historical narrative, and claim instead that the account contains 'literary clues' which point to its being symbolical rather than literal. One is the occurrence of numbers with symbolic significance. Another is the artistry, symmetry and ordered structure of the narrative, with three days of 'separation' followed by three days of 'adornment'. Another is the various lessons which the account teaches, such as the errors of certain pagan myths, and the error of worshipping the sun, moon and stars. There are other arguments also, but they are no more effective.

In answer, let me repeat three points made earlier: First, the grammatical structure of the Hebrew is that of *consecutive narrative prose*, not poetry, and in the context of Genesis and the rest of the Bible, it is clearly *historical* narrative. Second, the Old Testament, the New Testament and Jesus himself regarded the early chapters of Genesis as *history*. Third, before the rise of long-age geology and the theory of evolution, most exegetes (including all the Reformers and nearly all the Early Church Fathers) understood the early chapters of Genesis to be history.

As for the numbers with symbolic significance, the ordered structure, and the various lessons which the account teaches: all these are fully compatible with the account's historicity. God has the power to create in any way he wishes, and by choosing to create in that particular way, he was teaching certain lessons. These features do absolutely nothing to prove that the account is figurative.[1] The same theological message is conveyed whether the account is figurative or historical—*but the message is much more powerful and authoritative if the account is historical.* If the account is symbolical only, it is mere rhetoric. The message is not backed up by the historical facts. Worse than that, the message is a sham. It is a false message. A vital part of the message is that God's original creation was flawless—absolutely perfect—whereas the *reality* (if there were millions of years of violence, disease and death) is that it was very far from perfect.

Supporters of this theory say also that the creation account is the product of an ancient Near Eastern culture, and that it is naïve to think it is meant to be taken as literal history. They say, quite rightly, that we must discover what it meant to the original readers. However, we must remember that God himself inspired the record, that it is foundational to the whole Bible, and that it is meant to be understood by all people in all ages—not just the original readers. Most of us do not have the privilege of knowing Hebrew, or the ancient cultures of the Near East. But we do have access to the Old and New Testaments, and the teaching of the Creator himself, Jesus Christ. And, as mentioned already, an important principle of interpretation is that the best interpreter of Scripture is Scripture itself. If we want to know what the creation account meant to its original readers, the best place to look is the Bible itself.

Framework theorists notice the frequency in ancient Near Eastern texts of the pattern 6 + 1, and they inform us that this means the author of Genesis 1 was using a stereotype from his cultural milieu. But a more biblical understanding, I suggest, is that Genesis 1 is the *source* of this pattern—just as the biblical account of the Flood is the *original* account, and the Babylonian Flood texts are corrupt later versions. There is good reason to believe that Genesis 1–11 is very ancient indeed—much more ancient than any other Near Eastern text.[2] When Moses compiled the book of Genesis, he used documents which were already very ancient. In fact, many of us believe that the original account of creation was revealed to Adam by the Creator. No human being witnessed the creation; so this revelation had to come from the only eyewitness, God himself.

Note

1. Literary devices are common in the *prose* of both biblical and ancient secular writing. **M. Kay**, On Literary Theorists Approach to Genesis 1: Part 2', in *Journal of Creation*, **21**(3): 93–101, 2007.

2. See, for example, **Bill Cooper,** *After the Flood* (Chichester: New Wine Press, 1995). His research has revealed the astonishing accuracy and antiquity of the Table of Nations in Genesis 10–11.

Problems

There are quite a number of problems that Bible-believing Christians have with accepting Genesis 1–11 as straightforward, historical narrative. Some problems are biblical, and some are scientific or archaeological, etc. The problems concern mainly the creation of the world and universe in six literal days just over 6000 years ago, the absence of carnivory and death, the Garden of Eden story, and Noah's worldwide Flood.

I am well aware of these apparent problems. It was partly because of them that I myself was an old-earth creationist for much of my life. I have found, however, that these questions do have answers, although because our knowledge is limited, we do not know the full answer to every question. As far as the scientific and archaeological problems are concerned, there has been an amazing increase of knowledge and understanding over the last few decades. I have come to believe, in fact, that there are much greater problems with the various 'old-earth' theories than with taking Genesis 1–11 as straightforward history.

Much has been written about these things, but I cannot go into much detail in a book of this size. All I can do here is list some general principles, and focus very briefly on two of the problems. For further reading, I recommend *Refuting Compromise* by Jonathan Sarfati, who is an apologist and PhD scientist. This scholarly work is directed primarily against the theory of progressive creation, but deals with many of these problems. A helpful book written in a more popular style is *The Creation Answers Book*, edited by Don Batten, also a PhD scientist, and published by Creation Ministries International. Many other books and articles are available, including those on creationist websites such as creation.com, www.answersingenesis.org, www.icr.org, www.csm.org.uk and www.biblicalcreation.org.uk.

Underlying reasons

Here are some of the underlying reasons why many Christians in the Western world have difficulty accepting that Genesis 1–11 is straightforward history. First, they have been led to believe that such an interpretation is incompatible with the facts of science. But the theory of evolution and billions of years are not *facts* of science. They are fallible *interpretations* of the scientific evidence.

Second, many people fall into the trap of thinking *naturalistically*, as the world does. They try to explain the original creation naturalistically, whereas the Bible depicts it as a series of awesome, stupendous miracles. There is nothing 'natural' or 'normal' about the creation of a whole universe in six days! When I understood this and accepted it, I found that many things became clearer to me.

Third, Genesis 1–11 deals with extraordinary and unique events which are not part of normal experience now. Again, many people are trapped into thinking naturalistically, and they refuse to accept that these events were historical because they do not happen today. They seem to forget that there were times in history, such as the time of the Exodus, when extraordinary, unique, miraculous things happened. Is it too hard to believe that such things happened when the world began?

Fourth, many people assume that the original, pre-Fall world was virtually the same as the world we live in now. They seem to be unable or unwilling to get their minds round the concept that the original world before the Fall was *a completely different kind of world.* It was a world which we cannot fully comprehend or imagine, because the only kind of world we know is the one we live in now. The whole creation was radically changed by the curse.

Fifth, there is a failure to comprehend that God is truly omnipotent. If he had wanted to, he could have created the entire universe in an instant. Also, he could have created a completely different kind of world, in which the balance of nature did not depend on carnivory and death. Charles Templeton was absolutely right to say that an omnipotent and loving God should have been able to do this. The Bible indicates that this was exactly what God did—so why can't we believe it?

The days of creation
An entire chapter is devoted to this subject in Sarfati's *Refuting Compromise*. All I can do here is deal with a few points briefly.

One 'problem' is that the account says God created the sun, moon and stars on the fourth day. Clearly, therefore (so it is said), the days cannot be literal, solar days. 'Day-age' theorists try to preserve the historicity of the account by saying that it means the sun, moon and stars *became visible* on the fourth day. However, this cannot be correct, as the Hebrew clearly means that they were *made* on the fourth day.[1] 'Literary framework' theorists, of course, simply say that it proves that the days are not literal days, and that the order of creation is not meant to be taken literally.

The biblical answer is that the account makes it perfectly clear that they were *literal* days, but the first three days were not normal *solar* days. All that is needed for a twenty-four-hour period of day and night is a rotating sphere and a directional light source. Both were there. The creation of the sphere, which must have been rotating, is recorded in Genesis 1:1–2, and the creation of the light source is recorded in 1:3–5: 'Then God said, "Let there be light"; and there was light … and God divided the light from the darkness. God called the light Day, and the darkness he called Night.' *This light was not the sun, because the sun was created later.* We are not told the exact nature of the light source; but we do not need to know. Remember that the creation of the universe in six days was *miraculous.* We do not have to explain it naturalistically.

Why did God take six days to create the universe, when he could have done it in an instant? The answer seems to be in Exodus 20:8–11, where it is stated, 'For in six days the LORD made the heavens and the earth, the sea, and all that is in them, and rested the seventh day. Therefore the LORD blessed the Sabbath day and hallowed it.' God accommodated himself to man, and set us an example for us to follow.

And why did he create things in the particular order in which he did create them? I suggest the following:
- The fact that the earth was created *first*, and that the sun, moon and stars were created *afterwards*, shows the *primary* importance of mankind and this world, and the *secondary* importance of the rest of the universe. Amazing though it is, the latter was created for *our* benefit (Genesis 1:14–19). God confirmed this

when he came down into this world and identified himself with the human race in the person of Jesus. Incidentally, remarkable new evidence is coming to light that our own Milky Way galaxy is literally at or near the centre of the universe.[2] The very idea of this is anathema to secular humanists!

- The fact that the heavenly bodies were created on the fourth day, and that the sun and moon are simply called 'the greater light' and 'the lesser light', conveys the message that they are not deities, and they should not be worshipped! Incidentally, the almost casual way in which the account says 'He made the stars also' points to his omnipotence. That little phrase refers to the entire universe with its billions of galaxies! (Concerning the apparent problem of distant starlight, see Chapter 5 in *The Creation Answers Book*[3] and *Starlight, Time and the New Physics*, by John Hartnett[4].)

- As mentioned earlier, the beautiful symmetry and order of creation, with its inbuilt mathematics, reflects God's wisdom, power and perfection. Creation which sprawled over billions of years, involving billions of deaths, would be the exact opposite—it would be imperfect, messy, cruel, haphazard, inefficient and wasteful.

Carnivory and death

There are obvious problems with the teaching that there was no carnivory and death (of men and animals) in the original creation. Many animals are marvellously designed for a carnivorous way of life. Predators maintain the balance of nature. Without predatory activity and animal death, the world would become overcrowded very rapidly, resulting in mass starvation. And what about insects and other lowly forms of animal life? There are a number of possible answers, but the main ones are indicated above in the fourth and fifth 'Underlying reasons'. Incidentally, the problem of overcrowding applies to human death too—but the Bible teaches very specifically that human death *was a consequence of Adam's disobedience*.

A different kind of problem is that, in some places, the Bible seems to approve of predatory activity. Henri Blocher (a literary framework theorist) wrote, '… the speeches of God in the book of Job exalt the terrifying beauty of the beasts of prey as God's work (Jb. 38:39ff.; 39:26ff. and the description of Leviathan in Jb.

41).'[5] That is true, but it does not prove that such beasts in their present form were part of the original creation. Is it likely that 'terror' was part of the original creation? The present creation is God's work, and is utterly awesome; but it is very different from the original creation. It is a creation which has been subjected to 'futility' and 'corruption' (Romans 8:20–21). Genesis 1:29–30; 9:3 and Isaiah 11:6–9; 65:17–25 indicate very clearly that predatory activity is not the ideal. The Bible also praises God for giving victory in battle; but that does not mean that war is good.

One argument is that animals have a lower level of consciousness than humans, and therefore do not suffer greatly, especially in the wild. Also, it is said, the concept of animal suffering is really just a matter of Western sensibility, as most people in the world are not bothered about it. In answer:

- It is a scientific fact that animals do suffer, however much or little that may be.
- Isaiah 11 and 65 (which were inspired by God and written by a Jew) make nonsense of the idea that it is merely a matter of Western sensibility.
- One might as well say that the campaign to abolish slavery was a matter of Western sensibility. Most people accepted slavery as normal until evangelical Christians fought to abolish it.

Notes

1. **J. Sarfati,** creation.com/how-could-the-days-of-genesis-1-be-literal-if-the-sun-wasnt-created-until-the-fourth-day
2. **D. R. Humphreys,** creation.com/our-galaxy-is-the-centre-of-the-universe-quantized-redshifts-show
J. Hartnett, creation.com/images/pdfs/tj/j18_1/j18_1_9.pdf
3. See creation.com/images/pdfs/cabook/chapter5.pdf
4. For a review of this book, see creation.com/starlight-and-time-a-further-breakthrough
5. **H. Blocher,** In the Beginning, p. 42.

Science

It is important to understand that all scientists deal with exactly the same scientific facts or observations. The difference between biblical creationists and secular scientists is the way in which they *interpret* those observations. The layperson tends to imagine that research scientists are totally objective in their work; but that is a myth. All scientists have paradigms or interpretive frameworks, rather like a pair of spectacles, through which they look at the evidence. Secular science's interpretive framework is *naturalistic.* Their very definition of 'science' excludes God. This is what a leading evolutionary geneticist, Professor Richard Lewontin, wrote:

> We take the side of [evolutionary] science in spite of the patent absurdity of some of its constructs ... in spite of the tolerance of the scientific community for unsubstantiated just-so stories, because we have a prior commitment, a commitment to materialism [the belief that matter is all that there is] ... Moreover, that materialism is an absolute, for we cannot allow a Divine Foot in the door. [1]

This means that secular science has already made up its mind that macro-evolution (the molecules-to-man kind of evolution) and 'billions of years' are facts *before* it has looked at the evidence. *It will never accept special creation, however strong the evidence in its favour.*

Biblical creationists have a very different interpretive framework. They believe that the Bible is the inerrant word of God and is trustworthy, not only in spiritual matters, but also in matters of history and science. This does not mean, as explained earlier, that they are wooden literalists. They recognize different forms of literature, such as poetry, metaphor and hyperbole. But if God has given us information about origins *that is clearly meant to be understood as real history*, then the evidence should be interpreted in the light of that information.

It is important also to understand that there are two kinds of science—*operational* science and *origins* science. 'Operational science' deals with the material universe *as it is now.* It is the kind of science which put man on the moon. In this kind of science, the scientist's interpretive framework makes little difference. There are many biblical creationist scientists, such as Professors Andy McIntosh and Stuart Burgess, who are involved in this kind of work. But 'origins science' tries to work out what happened *in the past*. It is impossible to recreate the past and perform experiments upon it. So it is a very much more speculative and less exact science, and the way in which a particular scientist interprets the evidence depends very much on his or her 'interpretive framework'.

The public is brainwashed into thinking in terms of evolution and billions of years; so most find it hard to imagine that anything else is possible. However, increasing numbers of Christians are discovering to their surprise and joy that the evidence can be explained in an entirely different way—in accordance with God's Word. And very often the evidence fits the biblical picture *much better* than the secular one. In fact, much of the evidence is strongly *against* evolution and billions of years. Many things are not fully understood yet, but fruitful scientific research is being done, and new discoveries are being made all the time. I can mention only a few points here; but many resources, such as books and DVDs, are available on this subject, and there are also excellent articles on creationist websites. Note that many different scientific disciplines are involved, as well as other disciplines like archaeology.

Incidentally, biblical creationist teaching has borne good fruit spiritually, as well as scientifically. Through it, many have come to faith in Jesus Christ for the first time, and many have been strengthened in their faith. Evolutionists claim that it would hinder the progress of science if creationism were adopted generally; but that is the opposite of the truth. Many of the founders and pioneers of modern science were Bible-believing Christians who took Genesis to mean what it says. By contrast, the theory of evolution has been of no benefit to humanity whatsoever, either scientifically or spiritually. It has borne much evil fruit, as described earlier, and there is good reason to believe that it has actually *hindered* the progress of science.[2]

Noah's Flood
The worldwide Flood of Noah's day is the key to understanding the geography

and geology of today's world from a biblical perspective—and also the biblical *timescale* of just over 6000 years since the creation. 'Flood geology' says that Noah's Flood was a gigantic cataclysm of unimaginable magnitude, causing huge changes to occur rapidly over a short period of time. Most of the rock layers were laid down and most fossils were buried during and after the Flood—and there is powerful evidence that this is indeed what happened. As well as the effects of water, there was enormous volcanic and tectonic[3] activity—indicated in the Bible by 'the fountains of the great deep' breaking up. The whole surface of the planet was reshaped. Most present-day mountains were pushed up during and after the Flood. Changes were made in days and months which uniformitarians say took place over millions of years.

The Flood was so cataclysmic and destructive that Peter compared it with the destruction of the world by fire at the end of the present age (2 Peter 3:3–13). In fact, the Bible makes it clear *in several different ways* that Noah's Flood was a cataclysmic, worldwide event. For example:

'all the fountains of the great deep were broken up';

'all the high hills under the whole heaven were covered … and the mountains were covered' by the water for many months;

a gigantic ark was built for Noah's family and the animals—completely unnecessary if it was a local flood;

God promised that there would never be such a flood again. If it was merely a local flood, God has broken his promise many times.

It is important to understand that the Bible's description of the Flood is completely incompatible with the secular, old-earth interpretation of the geological record. An event of this magnitude must have reshaped the surface of the planet, and must be responsible for most of the world's geological features. Note that there is powerful evidence for the Flood not only in geology, but also in mankind's collective memory—in the form of many Flood legends all over the world.[4]

Biblical creationists believe that the volcanic and tectonic activity caused warming of the oceans but cooling of the climate owing to ash in the atmosphere, and that this led to massive precipitation of snow, and an ice age which lasted about 700 years. (This is relevant to the interpretation of ice-cores, which are said by secular scientists to be proof positive of vast ages.[5]) Conditions were harsh and unstable for a long time after the Flood, but gradually settled down. We have hints of this in the book of Job, which probably dates from the period before Abraham. There are more references to ice and snow in Job than in any other book of the Bible. Also, his descriptions of behemoth and leviathan sound like a dinosaur and a creature called *Sarcosuchus imperator*. The latter was a kind of giant crocodile, known from its fossil remains.

Dinosaurs and carbon dating

What about dinosaurs? Secular scientists tell us that they died out sixty-five million years ago. Biblical creationists believe not only that they were contemporaneous with man, but also that they were on the ark, and became extinct *after* the Flood. (There was no need to take the very large adult dinosaurs on the ark, as small, young ones were adequate, and most dinosaurs were small anyway.) There is a good deal of evidence for this in legends, eyewitness accounts, carvings and cave paintings, and also in science. In particular, in 2005 there was a discovery of *Tyrannosaurus rex* bones containing soft tissue *which was still elastic*, with blood vessels and blood cells.[6] An article about this was written by Carl Wieland.[7] He pointed out the fairly obvious implication that these bones could not be seventy million years old. Obvious, that is, to those who are not ideologically committed to the theory of evolution and billions of years. This article naturally provoked a furious reaction from the secular scientists. A further article was written by Wieland and Menton in late 2005.[8] Like the first article, it contains striking photographs of the soft tissue found in the bones. These pictures can be seen in full colour at the website address given in note 7 (C. Wieland) below.

Carbon-14 is the radioisotope dating method which is most familiar to non-scientists. What most people have *not* heard is that it provides very strong evidence that the world is only a few thousand years old. Radioactive carbon-14 has a short half-life of only 5,730 years. Any carbon-containing materials that are truly older than 100,000 years should not contain detectable carbon-14. And yet carbon-14 has been found in many different materials throughout the earth's strata, from the top to the bottom. This includes organic remains like fossils, petrified wood, shells, whalebone, coal, oil and natural gas, as well as inorganic materials like marble, graphite and calcite. These samples are from all around the world and from all depths. The detected carbon-14 atoms simply should not exist in these materials if they are millions of years old. Most recently, carbon-14 has been found in diamonds, which are typically assumed to be many millions, if not billions, of years old. Twelve diamonds from different parts of Africa were tested, and all contained carbon-14. The great strength of bonds in diamonds means that contamination is simply not a possibility.[9]

Of course, secular scientists 'know' that the world and universe are billions of years old, and that the last *Tyrannosaurus rex* walked the earth many millions of years ago; so no evidence will ever convince them otherwise. They have attempted to explain away the above (and other) evidence, but the fact remains that there is powerful evidence that the world and universe are only a few thousand years old, just as the Bible says.

Not by chance!

Not by Chance! is the title of a book by a Jewish PhD scientist named Lee Spetner. He was a university academic for most of his life, and was an expert in physics, biophysics and information theory, with a special interest in evolution. In his book he makes it clear that genetic mutations always lead to a *loss* of information. No mutation has ever been observed which leads to an increase of information or complexity.[10] It is absolutely essential to the theory of evolution that there has been a massive *increase* of genetic information. The only mechanism that evolutionists can think of is 'mutations', which are genetic copying mistakes. The experimental evidence indicates therefore that macro-evolution has not occurred, does not occur and cannot occur—unless God causes it to occur by a continuous series of miracles. But the whole point of the theory of evolution is that it is a *natural* process, not a supernatural one. So 'theistic evolution' really makes no sense. In any case, the experimental evidence indicates that God is *not* causing genetic information and complexity to increase.

Evolutionary scientists point to the visible changes in the living world which are going on all around us, and they tell us that these changes are examples of evolution in action. Darwin's finches are a good example. (On the Galapagos Islands Darwin noticed that there were several different species of finch, and he deduced that all were descended from a single pair.) But this is not vertical 'macro-evolution'. That is, it is not the 'molecules-to-man' kind of evolution. It is a consequence of natural selection, but is simply horizontal 'variation' or 'diversification'—sometimes called 'micro-evolution'. There is a fundamental difference at the genetic level between these two kinds of 'evolution'. Macro-evolution would require a massive *increase* of genetic information and complexity. In micro-evolution there is absolutely *no increase* of genetic information. There is only shuffling, sorting, degradation and *loss* of genetic information. (This is always true, even when new varieties are classified as new species.) There is an increasing 'load' of harmful mutations in the genes, and information is constantly being lost; so the general trend is *downhill*, not uphill. In fact, genomes are deteriorating so rapidly that all life would be extinct by now if it began very much more than thousands of years ago.[11] The evidence accords fully with the Bible's teaching that the world and universe were created perfect a few thousand years ago, and are now *decaying*.

Although adaptation and variation go on all the time, no new 'kinds' of organism are being created. The Genesis 'kind' (Genesis 1:11ff.) seems to be equivalent to a genus or family in most cases; but sometimes it is a species. There is much variation *within* each kind, but, true to the biblical account, one kind never changes into another kind. Incidentally, biblical creationists prefer not to use the term 'micro-evolution'. That is because it is misleading, and it perpetuates the myth that micro-evolution is the same kind of evolution as macro-evolution, but on a smaller scale.

However, there is worse to come from the evolutionists' point of view. Even if mutations and natural selection *could* cause genetic information and complexity to increase, this could not occur unless a cell and its genes existed in the first place. And that is an insuperable obstacle, because it is impossible for life to arise by chance. The simplest form of true life is a single-celled organism; but molecular biologists have discovered that the cell is a computer-like machine of staggering complexity and sophistication. It is many times more complex and sophisticated than any machine designed and built by man. Michael Denton, a non-Christian molecular biologist, has estimated that if we knew how to build a machine as complex as the cell, it would take at least *one million years* to build one cell—working day and night, and churning out the parts on a mass-production basis.[12] He wrote: 'Alongside the level of ingenuity and complexity exhibited by the molecular machinery of life, even our most advanced artefacts appear clumsy. We feel humbled, as neolithic man would in the presence of twentieth-century technology.'[13]

The sheer complexity of the cell is not the only reason why it could not have arisen by chance. There are several reasons, another being the fact that it contains coded information (huge amounts of it). According to Werner Gitt, this kind of information cannot arise by chance. It can be created only by intelligence.[14] (Werner Gitt specialized in information technology, and was Director and Professor at the German Federal Institute of Physics and Technology.) And of course there are countless organisms vastly more complex and wonderful than a single-celled organism. It is the very simplest form of true life. Denton continues: 'In terms of complexity, an individual cell is nothing when compared with a system like the mammalian brain … Because of the vast number of unique adaptive connections, to assemble an object remotely resembling the brain would take an eternity, even applying the most sophisticated engineering techniques.'[15]

The secular evolutionists' idea that the universe created itself out of nothing and eventually produced man is simply ludicrous. It is irrational. Quite apart from anything else, it violates two of the most fundamental laws of physics—the first and second laws of thermodynamics. Secular scientists believe *by faith* that the universe created itself out of nothing, and that life arose by chance; but it is not a rational faith. It is not science. It is an atheistic religion—a fact recognized even by some of its own adherents.

'For since the creation of the world his [God's] invisible attributes are clearly seen, being understood by the things that are made, even his eternal power and Godhead, so that they [men] are without excuse' (Romans 1:20). Christians also have faith; but it is a rational faith based on solid evidence. We can see the proof of God's existence, and of his power and wisdom, in this amazing creation. But more than that, he has revealed himself to us personally. He has spoken. He did this supremely when he came down into this world and lived among us as a human being. But he has done this throughout history also, through mighty acts of power and through his chosen servants. Through those servants, he has given us his written word, the Bible. Let us believe it and trust it, right from the very first verse!

1. **R. Lewontin,** 'Billions and Billions of Demons', in *The New York Review*, 9 Jan. 1997, p. 31.

2. **J. Bergman,** creation.com/textbook-tyranny
J. Sarfati, creation.com/dna-marvellous-messages-or-mostly-mess

3. **D. Batten,** creation.com/images/pdfs/cabook/chapter11.pdf
J. R. Baumgardner, ww.icr.org/research/index/researchp_jb_largescaletectonics

4. **R. Conolly and R. Grigg,** creation.com/many-flood-legends

5. **M. Oard,** creation.com/do-greenland-ice-cores-show-over-one-hundred-thousand-years-of-annual-layers

6. **Schweitzer, M.H., Wittmeyer, J.L., Horner, J.R. and Toporski, J.K.,** 'Soft-tissue vessels and cellular preservation in *Tyrannosaurus rex*', in *Science* **307** (5717):1952–1955, 2005.

7. **C. Wieland,** creation.com/still-soft-and-stretchy

8. **C. Wieland and D. Menton,** 'Answering Objections to Creationist "Dinosaur Soft Tissue" Age Arguments', in *Journal of Creation (TJ),* **19**(3): 54–59, 2005.

9. **De Young,** *Thousands ... Not Billions,* pp. 45–62.

10. **L. Spetner,** *Not by Chance!* (New York: The Judaica Press, 1996).

11. **J. C. Sanford,** *Genetic Entropy and the Mystery of the Genome* (New York: Ivan Press, 2005). John Sanford is a retired Cornell University Professor of Genetics and the inventor of the 'gene gun' process.

12. **M. Denton,** *Evolution: A Theory in Crisis* (Bethesda, MD: Adler & Adler, 1986), pp. 329–330.

13. Ibid. p. 342.

14. **W. Gitt,** *In the Beginning was Information* (Bielefeld: CLV, 1994).

15. **Denton,** *Evolution*, pp. 330–331.

About Day One:

Day One's threefold commitment:

- To be faithful to the Bible, God's inerrant, infallible Word;
- To be relevant to our modern generation;
- To be excellent in our publication standards.

I continue to be thankful for the publications of Day One. They are biblical; they have sound theology; and they are relative to the issues at hand. The material is condensed and manageable while, at the same time, being complete—a challenging balance to find. We are happy in our ministry to make use of these excellent publications.

JOHN MACARTHUR, PASTOR-TEACHER, GRACE COMMUNITY CHURCH, CALIFORNIA

It a great encouragement to see Day One making such excellent progress. Their publications are always biblical, accessible and attractively produced, with no compromise on quality. Long may their progress continue and increase!

JOHN BLANCHARD, AUTHOR, EVANGELIST AND APOLOGIST

Visit our website for more information and to request a free catalogue of our books.

www.dayone.co.uk